# THE FOURTH YEAR ARE ANIMALS

# THE FOURTH YEAR ARE ANIMALS

*Richard Tulloch*

The right of the
University of Cambridge
to print and sell
all manner of books
was granted by
Henry VIII in 1534.
The University has printed
and published continuously
since 1584.

*Cambridge University Press*

CAMBRIDGE

NEW YORK   PORT CHESTER

MELBOURNE   SYDNEY

Published by the Press Syndicate of the University of Cambridge
The Pitt Building, Trumpington Street, Cambridge CB2 1RP
40 West 20th Street, New York, NY 10011-4211, USA
10 Stamford Road, Oakleigh, Victoria 3166, Australia

© Cambridge University Press 1987

First published 1987
Third printing 1991

Printed in Great Britain by
GreenShires Print Ltd, Kettering, Northamptonshire

GR

ISBN 0 521 34934 6

**Performance**

For permission to give a public performance of *The Fourth Year are Animals* please write to Permissions Department, Cambridge University Press, The Edinburgh Building, Shaftesbury Road, Cambridge CB2 2RU.

**Acknowledgements**

This play has enjoyed quite a number of productions around Australia, both by professional companies and school student groups. Many of the actors and directors who have worked on the show have contributed lines and ideas to the script. I have shamelessly included the best of these in this version of the text, and I freely admit that many of the little gems came not from my typewriter but out of the mouth of an inspired actor. I thank them all, but especially the original cast – Christine James, David Kerslake, Jean Kittson and Ian White.

# ACT NOW PLAYS

Series editor: Peter Rowlands
Founding editor: Andrew Bethell

**Roots, Rules and Tribulations**   Andrew Bethell
**Closed Circuit**   Mike English
**Faust and Furious**   Anne Lee
**Czechmate**   Gerry Docherty and Bill Kinross
**Gregory's Girl**   Bill Forsyth
**Vacuees**   Bill Martin
**Easy on the Relish**   Andrew Bethell
**Fans**   Mike English
**Wednesday's Child**   Tony Higgins
**The Tree that holds up the Sky**   Paul King
**The Fourth Year are Animals**   Richard Tulloch
**Fit for Heroes**   Charlie Moritz
**Terms of Engagement**   Martin Dimery
**Do We Ever See Grace**   Noel Greig
**Rainbow's Ending**   Noel Greig
**Kidsplay**   John Lee
**Wolf Boy**   Peter Charlton
**A Nice Little Earner**   Arnold Evans
**Clean Up Your Act**   Mike English
**A Valuable Learning Experience**   Gillian Wadds
**Heroin Lies**   Wayne Denfhy
**Hard to Swallow**   Mark Wheeller
**King of Limbo**   Adrian Flynn
**Dags**   Debra Oswald

# ABOUT THE PLAY

Alan Howman is beginning his first year of teaching. Finding his 4F English class difficult to handle in the classroom he organises an extraordinary series of lessons for them. This leads to conflicts with other members of staff and with the students themselves. *The Fourth Year are Animals* raises questions about the relationship between staff and students, and what constitutes good teaching.

*       *       *

In 1983 Toe Truck Theatre, the Australian company which originally devised *The Fourth Year are Animals*, performed it at an international theatre festival in France. A woman approached me after the show and told me in broken English how much she had enjoyed it.
'It reminds me exactly of the school where I teach.'
'Oh yes,' I replied, 'and what sort of school is that?'
'A very ordinary school – in Brazil!'

It's nice to find that a play written for and about schools in Parramatta and Wagga Wagga, New South Wales, can have universal appeal, but it's also disturbing to think that schools are such difficult places the world over.

*The Fourth Year are Animals* aims to get students and teachers thinking and talking together about their schools and how they work. Why do schools so often turn into battlegrounds, as teachers and students try to get the better of each other? Is it possible for them to treat each other as equal human beings? Do teachers have to pretend to be always right in order to get respect? Can schools cater for students who need individual attention?

I find it depressing that many of the most talented student teachers who began studying education with me have now left the profession. Either they felt uncomfortable with the tough 'policeman' role they were expected to play as teachers, or they became frustrated with the difficulty of changing the system, or they felt that they were not able to make the best use of their talents in schools.

Most of the teachers who have stayed on in schools admit that they have made big compromises in order to survive. 'You have to act out being a bully in front of the kids'; 'I know kids are all different but I have to treat my class of thirty as if they're all the same'; 'You can't admit in the staffroom that you're having trouble with a class' . . .

And in discussions with students after our performances we discovered some puzzling attitudes. While most of them felt they would enjoy having teachers who gave them more freedom in class, they admitted they would give these teachers such a hard time that they would be forced to get tough again. 'Then why do you take advantage of them?'
'We can't help it – it's just fun.'

Some people believe that schools are becoming worse. They feel that discipline is too lax, that students don't respect teachers as much as they used to and that basic skills of literacy and numeracy are not being taught as effectively.

There can be no doubt that schools are changing, but I would like to think that the changes are by and large good. Better understanding between staff and students ought to lead to happier, more co-operative classrooms. I hope that *The Fourth Year are Animals* can contribute to this process.

*Richard Tulloch*

# CHARACTERS

*Students (Class 4F)*

KELLY*
THERESA*
ARTHUR*
BILL
TRACY
STEVE
Up to twenty other students

*Staff*

| | |
|---|---|
| ALAN HOWMAN* | a new teacher, enthusiastic |
| MARIE FORBES* | young, has been teaching for four years; an old friend of Alan's |
| LES WILLIS* | older, strict, has been teaching for about twenty years |
| SYLVIA HARRISON* | the headteacher |

JIM KEAVEN
JULIE FOSTER

* *The Fourth Year are Animals* was originally devised as a play to be performed by a small touring company. Only the characters marked by an asterisk are essential, and with minor reallocation of lines and some doubling up of roles it can be performed by a cast of four. The script contains notes indicating how this can be done.

## STAGE DIRECTIONS

There are two kinds of directions in this playscript. Those in **bold type** provide information that is essential to an understanding of what is happening in the play at that time. For a play-reading, these should be read by a separate reader.

Those in *italic type* are less essential stage directions and offer suggestions to assist with a production of the play on stage. In a reading they are best not read out as they will hamper the flow of the play, although those who are reading may find that some of these instructions offer help with the interpretation of their lines.

**Play duration** Approximately one hour.

# THE FOURTH YEAR ARE ANIMALS

**PROLOGUE**   KELLY, THERESA, BILL, STEVE **and** TRACY **enter. They are all aged about fifteen and look very tough and aggressive. They address the audience directly.**

*(Note: in a small cast production Kelly can perform the whole of this scene as a monologue.)*

KELLY   Hey, you want to see our school?

THERESA   It's really great!

BILL   We're getting this new building down in Brandon Street.

STEVE   Yeah, and it's got all carpet and science labs and that.

TRACY   And they dug up all the asphalt and put in all grass and trees and that.

ALL   Really great!

KELLY   No-one's been in it yet.

BILL   Oh, except some kids got in there last week, but they just busted in, you know, looking for stuff and that.

THERESA   And they got rid of that hut where they had the fire.

STEVE   Oh, you know, that portable classroom that new teacher painted all pink and green and that.

KELLY   Yeah, he just got it all painted and put up posters and then the kids burned it down. Well, he reckoned it was kids anyway. He really went berserk!

ALL  Really great!

TRACY  He's not coming back to school this year. He's in a mental hospital!
*(General disbelief from the others)*

No, honest – Mrs Harrison told Theresa Caretti's mother. He's having all these electric shocks. You know, where they put wires on your head and burn out bits of your brain to make you forget stuff.

THERESA  Yuk! How'd you be, eh? Like Dracula. No, not Dracula – who's that one with the bolts in his neck?

KELLY  Oh, Frankenstein, yeah.

BILL  Yeah, back at school again today. Start of the year's not so bad.

STEVE  You can really stir the new teachers.

TRACY  Always plenty of new teachers.

KELLY  Dunno where they get 'em all from.

**(The** STUDENTS **exit.)**

SCENE 1  **Music. There is an explosion of activity as the** STUDENTS **and** STAFF **arrive for the beginning of the school year.**

**KELLY, TRACY and THERESA gang up on ARTHUR, baiting him.**

**Through this mêlée comes ALAN HOWMAN, a new teacher. He is trying to follow directions written on a piece of paper. After a few false turns he meets MARIE, another teacher and an old friend. She guides him towards the staffroom. The STUDENTS exit.**

*(Music fades so that the conversation can be heard.)*

MARIE  You missed the pre-term staff meeting.

ALAN    There's a train strike. I rang the school.

MARIE   So how'd you get here?

ALAN    Hitched. Eight hours.

MARIE   Not bad going from Grantham. Have you been to the flat?

ALAN    Yeah. Found the key. *(He pats his pocket.)* Look, Marie, are you sure it's all right for me to stay at your place?

MARIE   Sure I'm sure.

ALAN    I mean, I know our mothers sort of fixed it up.

MARIE   My mother, you mean. Fix anything, Mrs Forbes.

ALAN    My mother was a bit . . . dubious.

MARIE   Thought I'd seduce her little boy, did she?

ALAN    No . . . yeah, something like that. But what if the kids found out that two of the teachers were, you know . . .?

MARIE   Kids talk anyway. Look, we're both teaching at the same school, you've got nowhere to stay in the city, I've got a spare room . . .

ALAN    But seriously, if you'd rather I found somewhere else . . .

MARIE   We'll see how it goes. You never know, we might get on really well.

        *(Alan is a bit embarrassed by this and she regrets the remark.)*

ALAN    What's the school like?

MARIE   I dunno. School's school.

ALAN    But you've been teaching here four years.

MARIE   Feels like four hundred.

ALAN    Do you like teaching?

MARIE   I don't know – I've never done any.

ALAN     But . . .

MARIE    You couldn't call what I do teaching. *(She rummages in her bag.)* Here, I've got a letter for you.

         *(She hands the letter to him.)*

         Open it quick – it's telling you what classes you're getting.

         *(Alan opens his letter. Marie looks over his shoulder.)*

         Oh that makes me angry! They always give the new teachers all the classes nobody else wants. Especially if they miss the pre-term staff meeting.

ALAN     Are they all so bad?

MARIE    Look at this. Monday to Friday, every morning, 4F English.

ALAN     And?

MARIE    I used to teach them in the Third Year. They're animals.

         **(Music. MARIE exits. ALAN sets up the room to be the head's office in the next scene, then exits himself.)**


SCENE 2   KELLY, TRACY **and** THERESA **enter.**

         *(Note: in a small cast production Tracy can be dropped and her lines given to Theresa.)*

KELLY     All right, if you don't believe me ask him yourself.

TRACY     He hasn't even got his licence!

KELLY     They were in his brother's car out near the heath. They weren't drinking or nothing.

THERESA   Then why'd they get picked up?

KELLY  I dunno. Two policemen just stopped 'em cause they didn't have their clothes on. They weren't doing anything.

(ALAN **enters and meets them.** TRACY **and** THERESA **giggle and move on. Alan catches** KELLY.)

ALAN  Excuse me – can you tell me where the office is?

KELLY  You a new teacher?

ALAN  That's right.

KELLY  What are you teaching?

ALAN  English, I think.

KELLY  Hasn't Mrs Harrison told ya?

ALAN  Is that the head?

KELLY  You want to see her?

ALAN  Yes, that's why I asked.

KELLY  You go down the end of this corridor, then there's double doors, that's the gym, and then you turn down to your left and that's her office.

ALAN  Thanks.

KELLY  Hey, what's your name?

ALAN  Alan . . . Mr Howman. What's yours?

KELLY  You been at a school yet?

ALAN  Sorry?

KELLY  You been at a school yet?

ALAN  Have I been teaching at a school, you mean?

KELLY  Yeah.

ALAN  Yes, I did some teaching practice while I was at college.

KELLY  This is your first job as a teacher, hey?

ALAN    Paid job, yes.

KELLY    Oh – hope we get you.

ALAN    You never know your luck.

(KELLY **meets her** FRIENDS **and they all exit.** ARTHUR **enters and stands waiting outside the head's office.** ALAN **moves on until he meets him.**)

Are you waiting to see Mrs Harrison?

ARTHUR    Yes, Sir.

ALAN    Is she on the phone or something?

ARTHUR    I dunno, Sir. You can go in if you like, Sir.

(ALAN **is about to enter when** MRS HARRISON **appears.**)

HARRISON    Hello, Arthur. Well, it didn't take you long to get into trouble, did it? Quarter to nine on the first day back. What have you been doing?

(ARTHUR **presents her with a grubby piece of paper.**)

ARTHUR    Mr Barker sent this note, Miss.

(She reads the note.)

HARRISON    And why were you doing that, Arthur?

ARTHUR    The toilets were still locked, Miss.

HARRISON    But you could have gone round to the other toilets in the yard. They weren't locked were they?

ARTHUR    Dunno, Miss.

HARRISON    They've just been planted, those trees. Have you any idea what they cost?

ARTHUR    No, Miss.

HARRISON    Well, it was a lot, Arthur. So next time, go to the toilet before you come to school. All right, love?

ARTHUR    Yes, Miss.

(ARTHUR **exits.**)

HARRISON  Poor old Arthur. Always someone on his back. I'm sorry, were you waiting to see me?

ALAN  That's alright. I'm Alan Howman. I'm a new teacher here.

HARRISON  Oh yes, Sylvia Harrison, sit yourself down.

*(Alan sits.)*

ALAN  I'm sorry I couldn't make it yesterday.

HARRISON  Oh, train strikes!

ALAN  Did you get my message?

HARRISON  Yes, we did, thank you. Well, it's a pity you missed the staff meeting, but better late than never. Now, what have we given you?

(ALAN **hands her his letter.**)

HARRISON  Oh yes, 4F English . . . And how would you feel about taking Third Year music?

ALAN  Music?

HARRISON  Just one class a week, on Tuesday afternoon.

ALAN  Well, I've never done any music.

HARRISON  That's a pity, but it's a time-tabling problem really. The only teacher with any musical background is Jim Keaven, who plays in some rock band, but he's got Personal Development on Tuesdays.

ALAN  All right, if there's no-one else.

HARRISON  Great, that would be a big help. Now did they show you where the staffroom is?

ALAN  I think I can find it again.

HARRISON  Then go and have a cup of coffee and prepare yourself for the onslaught.

ALAN  Thanks.

HARRISON  *(She offers her hand.)* Welcome aboard, Alan.

**(They shake hands, then both exit.)**


SCENE 3  KELLY **enters, carrying coffee and mugs. She enters the room and moves the furniture to convert it to the staffroom, then begins to dry the cups with a teatowel, looking with interest at the (imaginary) notices on the wall.** WILLIS, **a teacher of the 'old school', enters, carrying a briefcase and a pile of exercise books. He is accompanied by a younger teacher,** JIM KEAVEN. **They stop when they see Kelly.**

*(Note: in a small cast production Jim Keaven can be dropped, leaving Willis to reprimand Kelly.)*

KEAVEN  Kelly McCarrie, what are you doing in here?

KELLY  Miss Forbes told me to come and wash the cups, Sir.

KEAVEN  All right, hurry up.

**(KELLY exits. WILLIS and KEAVEN exchange glances – 'Kids are hopeless these days!' Willis sits to mark the exercise books.)**

WILLIS  I don't know what they teach kids in primary school these days. Too much plasticene and macramé and by the time they get to the Third Year, half the little maniacs can't read or write. *(He corrects a paper with relish.)* Can't spell 'rectangular' or 'isosceles' or 'prism'.

**(KEAVEN laughs and exits. ALAN enters and crosses to the coffee cups.)**

ALAN  Hi, like a cup of coffee?

**(WILLIS looks up and sees him for the first time.)**

WILLIS  What are you doing in here?

ALAN  Just making a cup of coffee.

(WILLIS **crosses to** ALAN **and grabs him by the scruff of the neck.**)

WILLIS  Where's your uniform?

ALAN  Sorry?

WILLIS  What's your name?

ALAN  Alan Howman.

WILLIS  And what class are you in?

ALAN  No, I'm Alan Howman. I'm a teacher here.

WILLIS  Oh. *(Willis extends his hand.)* Les Willis. Sorry about that.

ALAN  That's all right. I'll survive.

WILLIS  Teachers here usually wear ties.

*(Alan is wearing a rather flashy open-necked shirt.)*

ALAN  Oh.

WILLIS  Where are you from?

ALAN  Grantham.

WILLIS  Oh. Hope you're better than the last one we had down from there. Hippie. No control over the classroom at all. I walked in on one of his classes and he had all thirty-three of the little darlings lying down between the tables pretending to be ice lollies melting under the sun. Now I might be a bit old-fashioned but I can't see much educational value in that, can you?

ALAN  I suppose you'd have to see it in context.

WILLIS  Well, I did see it in context and I can tell you, if I were an employer I'd much rather take on a young person who could read and write than one who lay around all day pretending to be an ice lolly. Talk about youth unemployment!

(ALAN **is trying not to get drawn into the argument.**)

ALAN  Coffee?

WILLIS   Thanks.

(*Alan spoons coffee into a cup. Willis resumes his marking.*)

ALAN   Have you been teaching here long?

WILLIS   Pardon?

ALAN   I said, 'Have you been teaching here long?'

WILLIS   Mine's the brown one.

ALAN   Sorry?

WILLIS   That's not my cup.

ALAN   Oh. (*He finds the brown cup and tips coffee into it.*) Milk?

WILLIS   Black, thanks.

ALAN   Sugar?

WILLIS   Black.

ALAN   Where's the kettle?

WILLIS   There's an urn . . . but it's broken.

(WILLIS **produces a thermos flask from his briefcase. He pours for himself and** ALAN, **then indicates the bottom of his cup.**)

WILLIS   Got my name on it.

(ALAN **looks, then checks the bottom of his own cup.**)

That's a spare. I remember now – you're the music man, aren't you?

ALAN   Well, I'm supposed to be teaching music . . .

WILLIS   Good. Nothing against music.

ALAN   No, the kids usually like it. I suppose I'll have to start watching 'Top of the Pops'. INXS, Duran Duran, Throbbing Gristle . . .

WILLIS   I beg your pardon?

ALAN    'Throbbing Gristle'. It's a sort of post-New Wave jazz-rock-funk fusion.

WILLIS    Well, don't let it get out of hand. The little darlings always try out a new teacher, you know. What've you got next period?

ALAN    4F English.

WILLIS    Oh. Good luck.

(WILLIS **exits.** ALAN **waits, then exits too.)**

SCENE 4    CLASS 4F **enter. Their conversation continues as they walk around the corridors, unpack their schoolbags and finally enter the room and re-arrange the furniture to make it into a classroom, with chairs in a row and the teacher's desk in front.**

*(Note: in a small cast production this scene can begin with a conversation between Kelly and Theresa.)*

THERESA    Oh, he's not! Lots of people wear striped shirts *(or whatever Alan is wearing).*

BILL    Not with yellow trousers. *(He minces around, playing camp.)*

TRACY    *(To Kelly)* You were talking to him.

KELLY    He just asked me the way to the office, OK?

THERESA    What's his name?

KELLY    I dunno. I didn't ask him.

TRACY    How old is he?

KELLY    I dunno. He's a teacher – forty?

STEVE    You reckon he's a bit of alright?

KELLY    Come off it! He's a teacher!

(ARTHUR **enters.)**

BILL    Come on, Arthur, shake a leg!

KELLY       Been doing some gardening, Arthur?

STEVE       He was just watering the trees, weren't you, Arthur?

ARTHUR      Shut up!

THERESA     I tell ya who I do fancy, though.

KELLY       Who?

THERESA     Darryl Somers.

KELLY       Oh, yuk!

(ALAN **enters. He stops at the door of the classroom.**)

ALAN        Is this 4F English? Is that you?

(**No-one answers. They move silently to their places.**)

Sorry, I thought I'd better check . . . um . . . I'm Alan Howman.

KELLY       *(Whispers)* How, man!

*(There are giggles.)*

ALAN        All right, settle down. Anyway, I'll be taking you for English this year. Now I know . . . well I don't really know, but I assume that probably most of what you did in English last year involved quite a lot of spelling and grammar and other things that you may have found a bit boring . . .

STEVE       *To Kill a Mockingbird* – uuurrggghhhh!

*(More giggles)*

ALAN        All right, settle down. Now this year we'll be doing more literature, reading more books than you've been doing before . . .

*(Groans)*

But good books, which I think you'll like. And we might even have time to do some drama for a few sessions and other things like that.

(THERESA's **hand goes up.**)

Yes?

THERESA  Will we be doing essays, Mr Howman?

KELLY  How, man!

THERESA  Shut up!

ALAN  All right, settle down! Well, actually in a minute I'd like to get you to do some writing for me because I don't know very much about you and you don't know very much about me, although some of you I've met before like . . . *(to Kelly)* what's your name?

KELLY  Me?

ALAN  Yes, you.

KELLY  Annie . . . Lennox.

ALAN  Like Annie, here.

*(Mild hysteria from the class)*

And Arthur I met outside Mrs Harrison's office.

ALL  Oooooh, Arthur!

*(Arthur stands.)*

ARTHUR  Sir, her name's not really Annie Lennox, Sir. That's a singer . . .

KELLY  Shut up, Arthur.

ARTHUR  She's Kelly McCarrie.

KELLY  Jeez you're a dickhead!

(ARTHUR **shoves her and a fight begins.** ALAN **separates them.**)

ALAN  Alright, that'll do! Sit down, both of you!

*(They sit down.)*

Now let's get one thing straight. We're all going to be

together in this room for the whole year, whether we like it or not, and the only way we can make that tolerable is to at least try to get along with each other as best we can. Now, Kelly, I don't care if you want to have your little joke. You can call yourself Gertrude Gravelbottom or Betty Banana if you want to, it's all the same to me. And Arthur, I know you thought you were helping, but we're not going to get on with each other if we tell on each other all the time. I'll decide when the joke's gone far enough. OK?

KELLY    Sorry, Arthur. I'm sorry I called you a dickhead!

**(The scrap begins again.)**

ALAN    All right, settle down! This hasn't been a very good start, but look, I want to get you to do some writing . . .

THERESA    Is this a test, Mr Howman?

KELLY    How, man!

THERESA    Shut up!

ALAN    Yes, I think we've had enough of that joke, Kelly. No, it's not a test and there's no marks for it. All I'd like to see for the next twenty minutes or so, till the end of the period . . .

STEVE    Excuse me, Sir – there's only fifteen minutes left.

ALAN    Is that right?

*(General agreement)*

Right, I'll tell you what. Just for five minutes, get writing, just off the top of your heads, about anything at all – perhaps about the last day of the school holidays. All right?

*(No-one moves.)*

Start! Now!

*(Slowly they start to write. Alan paces up and down, then notices that Arthur is contorted, bent over his work.)*

Arthur, you don't write with your nose.

**(ARTHUR straightens up. THERESA tries to see KELLY's work.)**

THERESA  Oh, give us a look!

KELLY  No – get out.

THERESA  Oh, go on!

KELLY  Piss off!

ALAN  Settle down, you two.

KELLY  She's trying to look all the time.

ALAN  *(To Theresa)* Well, could you leave her alone? I'm sorry, what's your name?

ARTHUR  Theresa.

ALAN  All right, Arthur, remember! How are you getting on?

ARTHUR  Finished, Sir.

ALAN  *(Surprised)* Oh, let's see.

**(ARTHUR hands him his work. ALAN reads:)**

'Yesterday I played . . . Pic . . .' What's this?

ARTHUR  'Pac-Man', Sir. *(Arthur reads.)* 'Yesterday I played Pac-Man. My best score was six thousand eight hundred and ninety-eight. Then I went home.'

ALAN  Is that all?

ARTHUR  Yes, Sir. I didn't do anything else yesterday.

ALAN  *(Trying to be encouraging at all costs)* Good, fine . . . but perhaps you could make it even more interesting by telling us a bit about where you were playing Pac-Man or how you felt when you scored six thousand whatever it was. Have a go at it. There's still a few minutes left.

(ARTHUR **resumes his work.** KELLY **passes her paper to** THERESA**, who giggles.**)

Have you finished, Kelly?

(**He takes the paper from** THERESA. TRACY **rises and goes to leave the room.**)

ALAN    Where are you going?

TRACY    I'm lunch monitor, Sir.

(TRACY **exits.** ALAN **reads** KELLY's **paper.**)

ALAN    'There was a young teacher called Howman, Who thought sex was like milking a cow, man . . .'

KELLY    Well, you said we could write anything we liked, Sir.

(ALAN **tears up** KELLY's **paper as** ARTHUR **rises to read his newly-developed opus.**)

ARTHUR    'Yesterday I played Pac-Man. At the sports club. My best score was six thousand eight hundred and ninety-eight. That made me feel good. Then I went home.'

*(The bell rings. The class scramble for their bags and books.)*

ALAN    All right, you may go quietly.

*(They jostle each other.)*

*(Yells)* Don't push!!

(**The** STUDENTS **exit**)

(**Music.** ALAN **moves furniture to make Marie's flat.**)

SCENE 5    **It is late at night.** ALAN **sits at the kitchen table, working at a lesson plan.** MARIE **enters, drying a plate with a striped teatowel.**

MARIE    Alan, have you seen the TV guide?

*(He hands it to her and goes on working.)*

ALAN How does this sound? I walk in and start off reading a bit from *Lord of the Flies.* I've timed that at four and a half minutes. Then two minutes talking to your neighbour and ten minutes small group discussion about gangs and authority. Each group to write down three points about what makes a leader.

MARIE Boring.

ALAN Do you think the ten minutes is too long?

MARIE Alan, if you want to prepare lessons at night, fine, but I don't want to know about it, OK?

ALAN Sorry. Had a tough day?

MARIE *(Snaps)* Yes. I spend eight hours a day at that school, and when I come home I just want to relax.

ALAN Don't you have to prepare lessons?

MARIE I used to. But I soon found out there's too many things you can't predict. You just get them all involved in something and some kid farts.

ALAN And there goes your atmosphere.

(MARIE **treats this with the scorn it deserves and returns to the TV guide.**)

MARIE Oh, great – 'Creature Feature'!

ALAN What?

MARIE On TV – the late-night monster movie.

ALAN No time for television.

MARIE *(Reads)* 'The Curse of the Mummy's Tomb'. Three stars.

ALAN Sounds fantastic.

MARIE Oh come on, Alan. You have to relax some time or you'll go mad.

ALAN I'll relax when I've got a good lesson plan.

MARIE    Some of the best ideas for lessons come from late-night TV. *(She starts to go.)* The whole of 4F will be watching it, so why shouldn't you?

(MARIE **exits. Music from backstage as she calls:**)

MARIE    It's starting!

(ALAN **gives up and exits after her.**)

SCENE 6    **It is the following morning.** ALAN **enters bursting with enthusiasm, having had an idea for a brilliant lesson. He sets up his classroom, constructing a podium from desks and chairs. He turns on a cassette recorder which plays vaguely Middle-Eastern music. He removes his shirt and ties the striped teatowel around his head, suggesting Egyptian headgear. He opens a large book with colour plates about Egypt and displays it prominently. Finally he mounts the podium himself and stands with two large ostrich feathers held in his crossed arms.**

*(Arthur enters and stands amazed. Alan gestures with a feather, indicating that he should sit on the floor. As he does so, the rest of the class enter, Bill holding forth on the late-night movie . . .)*

BILL    . . . Oh, and when they took the bandages off the mummy's face and there was all that blood and bits of flesh hanging down!

THERESA    I thought I was going to have a nightmare.

KELLY    I did have a nightmare. I dreamed I was in this tomb and all these mummies with no eyes were coming to get me . . .

*(She stops as she sees Alan. He gestures them to their places on the floor. Kelly nudges Theresa and they do as he indicates.)*

*(Alan speaks gently and dramatically and against all odds manages to create a compelling atmosphere . . .)*

ALAN In ancient Egypt, when one of the great kings, one of the pharaohs, died, he was buried along with all his possessions. The Egyptians believed that death was like a journey from one world to the next. So they placed by the coffin of the pharaoh all the things he would need on that journey – food, clothing, sometimes even his servants and animals were buried along with him. So when archaeologists opened up these tombs they were able to build up a picture of the world the Egyptians must have lived in *(He displays colour plates from the book.)* . . . of their day-to-day life, and of the skill of their craftsmen in making precious objects of gold and silver.

**(Throughout all this, 4F have been silent, first out of curiosity at** ALAN's **behaviour, then becoming genuinely interested in what he is telling them.)**

I wonder what we've got at home that we would consider valuable?

*(Tracy's hand goes up.)*

Tracy?

TRACY I've got a brooch, Sir, that my grandmother gave me, and it's got all rubies, and it's silver . . .

ALAN Right, Tracy's got a brooch. Bill, what have you got that's valuable?

BILL *(Serious)* Me ghetto blaster, Sir.

ALAN Arthur?

ARTHUR Me bike, Sir. Dad ran over it yesterday.

ALAN Just for a moment, think about the thing you've chosen. Think about what makes it so valuable to you:

*(Pause while they do this.)*

Now if you'll come up to me I'm going to give each
of you an object, and I want you to imagine that this
object is very valuable.

**(They form a line in front of him. ALAN mimes placing
an object in each of their hands.)**

As you take your object, feel its weight, its texture,
and try to imagine what it might be. Think how
valuable it is.

**(When it is ARTHUR's turn, ALAN gets him to sit up on
the podium, holding the ostrich feathers across his
chest.)**

Now, I want us to imagine that Arthur is the pharaoh –
the great king over all of us. And our pharaoh has
died.

**(ARTHUR closes his eyes but remains sitting upright.)**

So what we must do now is bring our very valuable
objects and give them to be buried with our dead
pharaoh. So one by one can we do that?

**(KELLY comes up first. She gently places her imaginary
object in ARTHUR's hand. Then . . .)**

KELLY　He should be lying down, Sir, if he's dead.

ALAN　All right, Arthur, lie down.

*(Gently they lay Arthur on the podium.)*

KELLY　Just a minute, Sir. I got an idea.

**(KELLY runs from the room and exits.)**

ALAN　Kelly, where are you going?

**(She is gone, so he returns to the rest of the class.)**

Now think about our pharaoh. Think about what he
meant to us when he was alive. He was a king who
looked after his people . . .

**(KELLY returns with a roll of toilet paper and begins to
wrap ARTHUR up.)**

KELLY     Like in the 'Mummy's Tomb', Sir.

*(Alan has no option but to go along with her idea.)*

ALAN     As we are wrapping our king, we do it with respect for him, with honour and with love . . .

**(The** PUBLIC ADDRESS SYSTEM **crackles into life and a voice announces:)**

VOICE     Could I have your attention, please? The ladies in the canteen would like to advise us that as from next Tuesday the price of Cornish pasties will be thirty-three pence instead of thirty. Thank you.

**(Any atmosphere which had been created is now well and truly destroyed.)**

ARTHUR     Not on me mouth.

STEVE     We have to, Arthur, your majesty.

ALAN     We must be gentle with our king, with the body of our pharaoh . . .

**(Again the** SPEAKER **crackles.)**

VOICE     Sorry, teachers, listen once again. Another message from the canteen. Orange juice will no longer be available on Thursdays. Thank you.

*(Alan carries on valiantly.)*

ALAN     Our king has saved us from floods and fires, from famine and locust plagues . . .

ARTHUR     It's too tight!

BILL     Shut up, Arthur – you're dead!

*(Alan desperately tries to grab the class's attention again . . .)*

ALAN     Now we have to go out into the fields and perform the dance of death . . .

**(KELLY whispers to** TRACY **and** THERESA. **They move to exit.)**

Hey!

KELLY    Sir, we need more toilet paper.

ALAN    No, we've got enough. Now eyes this way a minute.

TRACY    We've got to do his legs, Sir.

KELLY    I'll get some from the boys' bogs!

(KELLY **runs from the room and exits. The** REST OF
THE CLASS, **apart from** ARTHUR, **follows.**)

ALAN    Kelly!

(ARTHUR **struggles.**)

ARTHUR    Can I get up now, Sir?

ALAN    No, just stay where you are, Arthur.

(ALAN **runs off after** 4F, **shouting:**)

Kelly, Theresa – come back here all of you!

(ARTHUR **is left alone, lying on the podium, swathed in
toilet paper.**)

ARTHUR    Sir . . . Sir? My nose is itchy, Sir.

(MRS HARRISON **enters. She stops when she sees**
ARTHUR.)

HARRISON    Who's that?

(ARTHUR **stands up, scattering toilet paper everywhere.**)

ARTHUR    Hello, Miss.

HARRISON    What are you doing, Arthur?

ARTHUR    I'm the king, Miss. I'm dead.

HARRISON    Where's Mr Howman?

ARTHUR    Don't know, Miss.

(ALAN **returns, shouting back behind him:**)

ALAN    Get back here all of you! We don't need any more

toilet paper! *(He comes face to face with Mrs Harrison.)*
We're doing Egypt. This is the Mummy's Tomb.
Arthur – put all this in the bin, please.

(ARTHUR **clears up the mess and exits.**)

HARRISON  And how is Egypt going?

ALAN  Fine, great . . . hopeless.

HARRISON  It looks like fun.

ALAN  Fun!

(**Together they demolish the podium and set up what will be the staffroom in the next scene.** ALAN **puts his shirt back on.**)

HARRISON  In my day, teachers never dreamed of any of this. It was chalk and talk and that was it.

(**A group of** STUDENTS, **including** KELLY, **runs past the door . . .**)

KELLY  Try the bogs by the gym! The boys have only got loose leaf!

(**They disappear.**)

HARRISON  Then on the other hand . . .

ALAN  I'm sorry about the riot.

HARRISON  It won't do, Alan. There are rules about keeping them in the classroom.

ALAN  It wasn't meant to happen.

HARRISON  Look, why don't you take them to the Flexi-area one period a week? Then you can do these . . . experiments without disturbing anyone else.

(WILLIS **enters, carrying a handful of empty toilet rolls which he dumps ostentatiously on the desk.**)

WILLIS  I thought Mr Howman might find a use for these next time he's doing creative drama.

(WILLIS **exits.**)

HARRISON  And that would save us all a lot of trouble.

(HARRISON **and** ALAN **exit, Alan giving the two-fingered salute with toilet rolls on his fingers. Music.**)

SCENE 7  ALAN **is working in the staffroom. He produces a newspaper clipping from his folder.** MARIE **enters holding a newspaper with a hole in the front page.**

MARIE  Hello, Sunshine, found another gourmet recipe?

ALAN  This was in the paper.

*(Marie pokes a finger through the hole.)*

MARIE  So it was.

ALAN  It's a special schools' exhibition at the Arts Museum.

(**He hands it to her. She reads:**)

MARIE  'Myths, Magic and Mummies – the Wonders of Ancient Egypt'. Sounds very educational. Thinking of going?

ALAN  I was thinking of taking 4F.

MARIE  4F?

ALAN  Yes, we've been doing that work on Egypt and it would fit in really well.

MARIE  You're a glutton for punishment.

ALAN  I just have to get them out of that classroom, Marie.

MARIE  It means spending the next three weeks filling in forms and chasing up kids.

ALAN  I'm a glutton for punishment.

MARIE  You want an excursion? Follow me. One, get the permission of your subject master; two, organise a bus; three, notes to the parents; four . . .

(MARIE **leads** ALAN **off during the last part of the**

conversation. **Without a break in the flow,** WILLIS **leads**
ALAN **on again. Both carry coffee cups.)**

WILLIS 'Myths, Magic and Mummies'?

ALAN Yes, well in 4F we've been doing that work on Egypt . . .

WILLIS 4F?

ALAN And I thought it would tie in really well with the sort
of thing . . .

WILLIS It's on a Thursday.

ALAN Yes.

WILLIS At 9.30.

ALAN Yes.

WILLIS 4F have got a maths test.

ALAN I know that, Les, but I thought that this week you
could let them off . . .

WILLIS Let them off???

ALAN Or organise the test on another day. Then I could take
them through my double English period, and because
it's not too far to the Museum I could have them back
by lunchtime.

WILLIS Alan, sit down.

*(Alan sits.)*

Alan, I'm sorry, I don't want to dampen your
enthusiasm, but when you've been teaching as long as I
have you'll come to realise that good teaching is based
on good routines. Now the way Fourth Year maths is
organised, I can teach the little darlings a unit of
material between Monday and Wednesday, test them of
a Thursday, and I can have the papers marked and
back in their hot little hands first thing of a Friday

morning. Now I may seem to you to be a bit set in my ways . . .

ALAN   Oh, no.

WILLIS   . . . but I've found over the years that the little darlings themselves appreciate this sort of routine. Now this 'Myths, Magic and Mummies' of yours is only going to upset the scheme of things. And when that happens, that's when the little piranhas take advantage.

ALAN   So it's 'no'?

WILLIS   I'm only thinking of the kids themselves.

ALAN   Look, Les, this excursion's very important to me, for . . . other reasons.

WILLIS   Yes?

ALAN   Well, as you probably know I've been finding 4F a bit . . . difficult.

WILLIS   Yes?

ALAN   And I thought if I could get them out of the classroom into a different environment . . .

(MARIE **enters.**)

MARIE   I said he'd be a problem.

WILLIS   Oh, so it's a conspiracy now, is it? Ganging up on old Les, eh?

ALAN   No.

MARIE   It's all right, Alan, I've got it all organised. Now it's the maths test that's the problem, is it?

WILLIS   It's not that it matters to me. 4F wouldn't want to miss a maths test. Some of them look forward to it all week.

MARIE   Well, we'll just have to see they're not disappointed, Les. Now Alan will have them back by lunchtime.

ALAN   It could be even earlier.

MARIE    Then they can have the maths test in Period 6.

WILLIS    I've got 3B in Period 6.

MARIE    Then take them to room 5 when you've got a free in Period 7.

*(Marie and Willis consult (imaginary) timetables on the walls.)*

WILLIS    Julie Foster's got her lot for RE in room 5 in Period 7.

MARIE    Then Julie can take her RE's to the Flexi-area and Jim Keaven takes his 5B Modern History to D block and keeps them there until mid afternoon.

WILLIS    That does mean there are four classes in D block in Period 6.

MARIE    Three.

WILLIS    Four. Max Gottlieb started a new Sixth Year debating group last Wednesday.

MARIE    Then how about this? Jim Keaven takes 5B Modern History to D block in Period 4. Julie Foster takes my 3J Geography to the Flexi-area in Period 6 and they can catch up on History when Jim's got them again in B4 in Period 3 in what would normally be Friday morning music. So instead of music with Alan, 5B go to swimming with Gary Callaghan, which takes us through till mid afternoon. That gives me a free, so I can go to the Flexi-area and babysit Les's 3B's while he goes to room 5 with 4F for the maths test.

*(Long pause as Willis studies the timetable, then . . .)*

WILLIS    All right. But if anything goes wrong, it's on your head.

*(Willis starts to leave, then looks at the bottom of his coffee cup. He notices that Alan is drinking from his cup, so comes back to change it.)*

ALAN    Thanks, Les.

(WILLIS **exits.**)

And thanks, Marie, I don't know how you got that organised.

MARIE    Neither do I. It doesn't make a word of sense, but by the time anyone finds out you'll be down at the Museum gawking at mummies.

ALAN    But what about when we get back?

MARIE    Don't worry. Kids love chaos.

(ALAN **exits.** KELLY **appears at the door of the staffroom.**)

KELLY    Miss . . .

(MARIE **looks up and sees that** KELLY **has crossed over the magic line onto the staffroom carpet, and stares at her. Kelly steps back.**)

Miss . . .

MARIE    Yes, Kelly?

KELLY    Can I have the key to the art room, Miss? I have to finish my mask.

MARIE    Kelly, it's lunchtime. You can finish your mask in Period 6.

KELLY    I just have to do the edges, Miss, then it'll be dry enough to paint. Oh, come on, Miss, just give us the key, I know where all the stuff is.

MARIE    No.

KELLY    Oh, that's not fair, Miss, you let Peter Ashe do his mask in there yesterday.

MARIE    Peter Ashe didn't throw clay all round the walls last time he was in there, Kelly.

KELLY    Miss?

MARIE    Nor did he use the palettes as ashtrays.

KELLY    That wasn't me done that, Miss, that was them other kids.

MARIE    It was you, Kelly.

KELLY    You calling me a liar, Miss?

MARIE    You are a liar, Kelly.

**(But she relents and holds out the keys to KELLY. Kelly sulks and refuses to take them. MARIE calmly pockets them and leaves the staffroom. Kelly follows her around the corridors.)**

KELLY    You don't trust me, do you Miss?

MARIE    I don't know, Kelly. If someone does trust you, you reckon they're a sucker, and if they don't, you reckon they're a bastard. You're just a bloody nuisance.

KELLY    You're always picking on me, Miss.

MARIE    It's not just me thinks you're a pest, Kelly.

KELLY    What's Mr Howman been saying about me?

MARIE    Mr Howman is one of the few teachers at this school who's really trying to do something for you lot. Now when someone's trying to build something up I don't like to see it wrecked, do you?

KELLY    *(Suggestive)* Is he a friend of yours, Miss?

MARIE    Don't even think of trying that one, Kelly.

**(MARIE exits. KELLY moves off the other way, then hides as she sees ARTHUR entering with ALAN in pursuit. She waits and overhears the first part of their conversation.)**

ALAN     Oh, Arthur, I still haven't collected your bus money for the excursion.

ARTHUR   No, Sir.

ALAN     Well, did you remember to bring it today?

ARTHUR   I don't think I'll be able to go, Sir.

ALAN   Oh, why not?

ARTHUR   I never go on excursions, Sir.

ALAN   Arthur, just step in here a minute, will you?

(*He leads Arthur into the staffroom and sits him down.*)

Why don't you ever go, Arthur?

ARTHUR   Dunno, Sir.

ALAN   Well, do you want to go?

ARTHUR   Yes, Sir.

ALAN   Did you take the note home to your parents?

ARTHUR   Yes, Sir.

ALAN   And what did they say?

ARTHUR   My Mum's in hospital, Sir.

ALAN   What's wrong with . . . what about your Dad?

ARTHUR   He does shift work, Sir. We don't see him much, me Dad.

ALAN   Do you have any brothers and sisters?

ARTHUR   No, Sir.

ALAN   So you're on your own when you go home at night?

ARTHUR   I can manage, Sir.

ALAN   Arthur, the school does have some money for . . . special cases. Do you want to go on the excursion?

ARTHUR   Yes, Sir.

ALAN   Then if you can get your Dad to sign the note, we'll organise something about the money. Can you do that?

ARTHUR   Yes, Sir.

(ALAN **lets him go. Outside the staffroom,** ARTHUR **meets** KELLY.)

KELLY   Hey, Arthur!

ARTHUR   What?

KELLY   Come here.

ARTHUR   What for?

KELLY   I just want to talk to you.

ARTHUR   You come over here.

(*Neither moves.*)

KELLY   What were you talking to Mr Howman about?

ARTHUR   The excursion.

KELLY   You going?

ARTHUR   Yeah.

KELLY   You never go.

ARTHUR   Mr Howman give me the money.

(ARTHUR **exits.** ALAN **comes out of the staffroom.**)

ALAN   Oh, Kelly, I still haven't collected your money, have I?

KELLY   My Mum said I couldn't go, Sir.

ALAN   Oh, why not?

KELLY   She said we couldn't afford it, Sir. Dad was laid off from the plant on Monday.

ALAN   Oh, that's no good. What does your father do?

KELLY   He just lies around the house all day, watching TV.

ALAN   No, I mean work.

KELLY   Oh, he's a boilermaker, Sir. Welds pipes and that.

ALAN   And is he often out of work?

KELLY   Quite often, Sir. We just have to wait for the dole cheque to come through. It'd be all right only he's just had to pay for my grandmother's funeral.

ALAN   I see. But you want to go on the excursion?

KELLY   Oh, yes, Sir. I'm really into Egypt and that. It's just I can't afford it.

(ALAN **smells a rather large rat.**)

ALAN   Well how about if I rang your mother . . .

KELLY   Oh no, Sir, don't do that!

ALAN   Why not?

KELLY   Mum'll be out all day. Visiting my grandad and making sure he's OK, you know.

ALAN   Is this really the truth, Kelly?

KELLY   Yes, Sir.

ALAN   All right, could your father sign the note? He's not dyslexic or crippled with arthritis or something?

KELLY   Sir?

ALAN   Don't worry, it's a joke. I'll get you the money if your father signs the note.

KELLY   Thanks, Sir. You're a good bloke, Sir.

ALAN   I hope your grandfather's all right, Kelly.

KELLY   We're all keeping our fingers crossed, Sir.

(ALAN **and** KELLY **exit. Music covers a swarm of activity as Alan leads 4F on the excursion. He leads them along the street, chats to** ARTHUR, **calls to stragglers to catch up and finally counts heads as they go through the Museum door.**

**All actors move the set to become the Museum. The frames which have been walls now become display screens and the desks become a 'glass case' in the shape of a sarcophagus.**)

SCENE 8   **The** STUDENTS **mill around as a** MUSEUM GUIDE,
**armed with a catalogue, points out the delights of the
exhibition.'**

*(Note: in a small cast production the guide can be cut and Alan
can read from the catalogue himself.)*

GUIDE   *(Reads)* 'The eyes of the body have been removed and
replaced with enamel eyes. The embalmer's next task
was to remove the brain via the nostrils with a curved
instrument.'

*(Kelly sticks a crooked finger up her nose.)*

KELLY   Like this, Sir?

*(Laughs from the class)*

ALAN   Come on, 4F, listen to this . . .

*(Kelly leans on the glass case.)*

GUIDE   'Many mummies have been found wearing rings and
other jewellery . . .'

BILL   My mummy does that.

**(The** GUIDE **moves the** CLASS **away. Some of them
follow the guide offstage.** ALAN **notices that** KELLY **is
leaning on the glass.)**

ALAN   Kelly, what does it say on that sign?

KELLY   *(Reads)* 'Please do not lean on the glass.' Oh, *this* glass,
Sir?

**(**KELLY **moves away from the case.** ARTHUR
**immediately takes her place leaning on the glass.)**

ALAN   Now there's still a few minutes left before the bus
comes. You may wander around and look at whatever
you like, but stay on this floor and don't touch!

**(**ARTHUR **moves away from the glass and raises his
hand.** KELLY **and** THERESA **sneak off for a quiet
smoke.)**

Those of you who've finished your question sheets can hand them in to me now. What is it Arthur?

ARTHUR  What are all those cockroaches for, Sir?

ALAN  What cockroaches?

ARTHUR  There, Sir, under the glass.

ALAN  Oh no, Arthur, they're scarab beetles. They had a sort of religious meaning for the Egyptians.

ARTHUR  Are they real ones, Sir?

ALAN  Yes, Arthur, they're over four thousand years old.

*(Kelly puts a cigarette in her mouth.)*

THERESA  Oh, come on, give us one!

KELLY  No, it'll make too much smoke. He'll see.

ARTHUR  Are they dead ones, Sir?

ALAN  I expect they are, Arthur.

THERESA  Oh, go on!

KELLY  I'll give you a puff of mine, OK?

THERESA  I paid for half of them!

KELLY  Sssh!

**(ALAN has heard this and crosses over to them.)**

ALAN  Ahem!

**(They look up guiltily. KELLY holds the unlighted cigarette in her mouth.)**

THERESA  We weren't doing anything, Sir.

KELLY  Just sucking on it, Sir.

ALAN  Kelly, I don't care if you want to ruin your lungs, but if you get caught smoking in here, I'm the one that gets the flak.

ARTHUR  Sir . . .

ALAN   Just a minute, Arthur.

ARTHUR   Why have they got pins through them, Sir?

ALAN   The Egyptians were very cruel to insects, Arthur. *(To Kelly)* Come on, hand them over.

*(She gives him the cigarette from her mouth.)*

And the rest of them.

KELLY   Sir . . .

ALAN   You'll get them back after school.

**(KELLY fishes the packet of cigarettes from her bag. As she does so a five pound note falls to the floor. Alan picks it up.)**

I thought you said you had no money for the bus.

KELLY   I didn't realise I had that, Sir. It was right down the bottom of me bag.

ALAN   Come over here. Theresa – get lost.

*(He draws Kelly aside.)*

Do you think I'm some sort of idiot, Kelly?

KELLY   Sir?

ALAN   Do you think I'm so stupid I like to stick my neck out for you to chop it off?

KELLY   I didn't know I had it, Sir. Honest.

ALAN   You're lying, Kelly. You know it and I know it. So how about we stop the stupid little games, eh? How about a bit of honest talk?

KELLY   What about?

ALAN   About anything you like, just so long as I get some straight answers, OK?

KELLY   OK.

ALAN   How about we talk about you?

KELLY   Why?

ALAN   Because I'm interested in you.

KELLY   Why don't we talk about you?

ALAN   All right, if you like, we'll do a deal. You can ask something about me and I'll ask something about you. But honest answers, all right?

KELLY   OK.

ALAN   Well go on. Your turn first.

KELLY   Can I ask anything I like?

ALAN   Yes.

KELLY   Are you married, Sir?

ALAN   No.

KELLY   But you live with that teacher, Miss Forbes.

ALAN   We share a flat together, yes.

KELLY   What else do you share?

ALAN   *(Defending grimly)* Food.

KELLY   And?

ALAN   Kelly, it's none of your business, but if you're asking me whether we sleep together, we don't.

KELLY   Oh.

ALAN   Kelly, she's a very good friend. She's been teaching a lot longer than I have and she helps me a lot. She helped me organise this excursion. Just because she's a woman and I'm a man doesn't mean we have to jump into bed together.

(THERESA **has crept back to eavesdrop.** KELLY **is aware of her presence but** ALAN **is not.**)

KELLY   Are you a poofter, Sir?

(ALAN **now realises that she has made this remark for**
THERESA's **benefit. He is furious.**)

ALAN   Theresa – get lost!

(THERESA **moves off.**)

KELLY   Well, are you?

ALAN   It wouldn't make any difference if I was but as it
happens I'm not.

KELLY   Oh.

ALAN   Anything else you want to ask? Any other nitty-gritty
little questions? *(Kelly shrugs.)* All right, now it's my
turn. Why do you go out of your way to bug me all
the time?

KELLY   I don't.

ALAN   Yes you do, and it's bloody annoying! When are you
going to grow up? How old are you?

KELLY   Fifteen.

ALAN   Fifteen. And what are you going to do for the rest of
your life? You've got the brains to go on with school,
you know. You could even go to university if you
really applied yourself. But what do you do? You
spend your whole life thinking up stupid little games
to amuse brainless twits like Theresa. What do you
think's going to happen to you, eh?

KELLY   Don't care.

(KELLY **begins to walk away from** ALAN, **but he**
**follows her, becoming angrier and angrier as she tries**
**to back out of the discussion. Other students, who have**
**been wandering around the Museum, are by now out of**
**sight.**)

ALAN   So you leave school. You've got no qualifications.

You'd be lucky to get a job working as a cashier in Woolworths. Is that what you want?

KELLY  I'll just get married, Sir.

ALAN  Oh yes, just get pregnant by the first pimply-faced twit you go with so that by the time you're seventeen you've got kids hanging round your ankles. Is that what you want? Is that what you really want? Or haven't you got the guts to answer that?

**(He grabs her and spins her around towards him, hurting her elbow.)**

KELLY  Finished, Sir?

**(He releases her. Both realise that he has gone too far.)**

ALAN  Oh, you think you're so smart, don't you?

**(She moves to exit.)**

Where are you going?

KELLY  Going for a piss, Sir.

ALAN  Kelly!

**(She stops. He gives her the five-pound note.)**

Buy some flowers for your Grandma's grave.

**(KELLY takes it and exits. THERESA and TRACY cross in front of ALAN, following Kelly.)**

ALAN  Where are you going?

TRACY  Going for a p... toilet, Sir.

ALAN  You've got two minutes.

**(THERESA and TRACY exit as ARTHUR wanders back on.)**

Come on, Arthur, the bus will be here.

ARTHUR  I haven't finished my question sheet yet, Sir.

ALAN  You've got ten seconds, Arthur.

(ARTHUR **exits. THERESA and** TRACY **return from the
toilets.)**

Theresa, where's Kelly? *(Theresa shrugs.)* Well go back
and tell her to get out here immediately!

(THERESA **exits.** ALAN **waits. Theresa returns.)**

Well?

THERESA   She's gone, Sir.

ALAN   What do you mean, 'Gone, Sir'?

THERESA   She must've climbed out the toilet window, Sir.

(THERESA **exits.** ALAN **moves in the direction of the
toilet and calls:)**

ALAN   Kelly? Kelly!

*(No answer)*

All right, everyone back on the bus!

(**Music.** ALAN **returns the set to the staffroom set up,
then exits.)**

SCENE 9   **Back at the school, the re-organised timetable has
caused total chaos.** STUDENTS **and** TEACHERS **wander
around.** JIM KEAVEN **meets** JULIE FOSTER.

*(Note: in a small cast production this exchange can be cut and the
scene picked up on the dialogue between Willis and Kelly.)*

KEAVEN   Julie, what are you doing?

FOSTER   Looking for 5J Modern History.

KEAVEN   I think I'm supposed to be looking after them.

FOSTER   No, Marie Forbes said I'm doing it.

KEAVEN   Did she say where?

FOSTER   Room 5, she said, but when I go down there's
three kids and seven teachers.

(BILL and STEVE **enter.**)

KEAVEN   Hey, there's some of mine. Where are you off to?

STEVE   Swimming with Mr Callaghan, Sir.

KEAVEN   No, you're not. You're coming down to D Block with me.

BILL   Oh, Sir . . .

FOSTER   Hopeless! I'm going to kill Miss Forbes when I catch her.

**(They all exit.)**

**(KELLY sneaks back on stage but is caught by WILLIS entering.)**

WILLIS   Kelly McCarrie! Where have you been?

KELLY   Excursion, Sir, with Mr Howman.

WILLIS   The bus came back an hour ago.

KELLY   I missed the bus, Sir.

WILLIS   You missed the bus?

KELLY   Sir, Mr Howman said that we could . . .

**(She is about to invent a lie, but ALAN enters.)**

WILLIS   What did Mr Howman say?

ALAN   It's my fault, Mr Willis. I gave Kelly permission to go to the Museum cafeteria and we must have forgotten about her. I'm very sorry about that, Kelly.

KELLY   Oh, that's all right, Sir.

**(She is amazed that he will put himself on the line for her.)**

ALAN   Well, you'd better run along. Whose class are you missing?

WILLIS   Mine.

ALAN   Hurry up then.

(KELLY **exits.**)

WILLIS  Well?

ALAN  I'm sorry about that, Les. These things happen.

WILLIS  These things shouldn't happen. Have you any idea of the chaos you've caused this morning?

(MARIE **enters, sees** WILLIS **and heads off in the opposite direction.**)

Miss Forbes!

(WILLIS **pursues** MARIE **off. Then Marie enters, with Willis following her and remonstrating with her.**)

WILLIS  Miss Forbes, the whole school is full of kids wandering around from classroom to classroom like lost sheep. Now I can take a joke as well as anyone else but when the whole school organisation becomes involved . . .

MARIE  Oh, give it a rest, Les.

WILLIS  It's not that it matters to me, but what about the kids? Now 4F will have to wait till Monday morning to get the results of their maths test.

MARIE  How will they stand the tension?

(ALAN **barely conceals a smirk.** WILLIS **turns on him.**)

WILLIS  And as for you, young man, it's an absolute disgrace. You're responsible for those kids for the full time they're under your care and control, if those are the right words for it, and if any kid goes missing, how does that reflect on the school?

ALAN  It's not the end of the world, Les, she was back by Period 7.

WILLIS  Let me tell you, son, if I were a parent whose child had been on that excursion I would be writing letters to the Department.

ALAN  Look, can't we get this into some kind of perspective?

WILLIS    In perspective?

ALAN    That excursion was an important part of those kids' education. With anything like that there's always an element of risk involved.

WILLIS    And what God-given right do you have to take risks with kids' lives? What right does any teacher have? 'Risk', he says.

ALAN    Just cool it, OK?

WILLIS    'Cool it'! Bloody hippie!

ALAN    All right, you've had your say. Now listen to me. From the moment I walked into this school everyone's been trying to tell me how to do my job. Now I didn't ask to be sent here. I didn't choose what classes I was going to teach. I didn't decide what sort of classrooms and tables and books and chalk and dusters we were going to use. I'm just the sucker thrown into the lions' den trying to do my best. Trying to do my best for a bunch of kids knowing full well they haven't had a choice either and half of them don't want to be here in the first place.

WILLIS    So what do you want? A democratic staff–student meeting every time we buy new set-squares?

ALAN    Les, unlike you I happen to believe in the potential of every one of those kids. I happen to believe in teaching and if I survive the next few weeks I might even get to like it. But kids don't come here for the teachers' benefit. We're here to help them and if we're not doing that we might as well burn the whole school down. I can't teach kids if I have no idea who they are, what they're like and what they want.

WILLIS    They don't know what they want.

ALAN    Have you ever asked them?

WILLIS    I know what they'd say - 'sex and drugs and rock and roll'.

ALAN   Don't pretend to be more stupid than you are, Les.

WILLIS   That's all most of the little darlings care about.

ALAN   If you think that, you're so obviously out of touch you don't deserve to be teaching!

**(Pause. WILLIS has obviously been hurt by this.)**

WILLIS   All right, I admit it. Poor old stick-in-the-mud Les is out of touch. He's too old. He's got no imagination. He still likes Beethoven better than the Rolling Stones. So what do you want me to do? Stick my head in a gas oven because I'm over forty? I'm not ashamed to say I don't understand kids at all. I don't even think I like them. But I've found one thing, Alan, that I *can* do bloody well. I can teach kids so that they go out of my classroom knowing more than when they came in.

ALAN   Whether they like it or not.

WILLIS   I don't care whether they like it or not. If they want a friend they can go out into the playground and find someone their own age to play with. All I need is their respect. I demand respect and I get respect. They may not like me, but I've been doing my best for those kids for twenty years. Are you still going to be here in twenty years' time? I don't think so.

**(WILLIS exits.)**

MARIE   Well, you handled that pretty tactfully.

ALAN   It's idiots like that that run the whole education system.

MARIE   Idiots make the best teachers.

ALAN   Don't give me that, Marie.

MARIE   It's people like Les who survive. They're the ones who go on teaching year after year. People like us only do it till we've saved enough to spend a year on the beach in Bali or buy a vegetarian restaurant.

ALAN   I'm not in it for the money, Marie.

MARIE   In that case you'll burn yourself out within a year. Teachers can't be brilliant and creative all the time.

ALAN   So what do you suggest? Your way? Les's way?

MARIE   They know where they stand with Les. He's everything they expect a teacher to be.

ALAN   We're not here to give kids what they expect. For Christ's sake, Marie, we live in a changing world. No-one knows what they're going to throw at us next and those kids have to learn to cope with that. The most important skill we can teach them is how to think for themselves when the unexpected happens.

MARIE   Come with me. I want to show you something.

(MARIE **leads** ALAN **across to the wall. Together they step through the frame and look at the students in the** AUDIENCE.)

*(Note: in some productions this has been felt to be too confronting and the scene has continued with Marie delivering her lines to Alan.)*

Why do you think kids come to school? Now that they're here what do they want to learn? 'Oh, don't know, Miss. You decide, Miss. Sit us down, shut us up and tell us what to do. We don't want to think about it.' It's a game. They play it and we play it and the whole thing runs very smoothly until someone tries to change the rules.

ALAN   But they're not learning anything.

MARIE   Yes they are, they're learning lots of things. How to think and speak and behave just like all the other kids. How to be one of the gang. They're learning how to take orders and obey instructions and how to cheat the system without being caught. They're learning that life is based on competition rather than co-operation and that what other people think of you is much more important than what you think of yourself. These are all very useful things you need to know to survive in the world. No employer would give you a job if you hadn't learned the basics at school. And that's exactly what education is all about.

(MARIE **exits.** ALAN **waits for a moment, then he exits too.**)

SCENE 10   **Music, heavy and jarring, as 4F enter. They are bullying** ARTHUR, **picking on him as they go around the corridors and enter the classroom. There they really turn the screws on Arthur, playing an ugly game of baiting him. Inside the classroom, furniture begins to be overturned. Arthur is reduced to pleading for mercy.**

ALAN **enters, now wearing a tie. He stops when he sees what is going on, then strides into the room and slams his books on a desk.**

*(Music cuts out abruptly as Alan screams:)*

ALAN   Sit down and shut up!

*(The students are shocked by his new-found violence. They move to their seats, righting the furniture.)*

If you're going to behave like children I'm going to treat you like children. We haven't made a very good start to this year, have we? We're going to change all that. Everybody stand up! In silence!

*(They stand. Alan continues quietly, seething:)*

Now I'll tell you what we're going to do. Very quietly we're going to walk out that door and form a straight line along the corridor. And when we're standing quietly we'll walk back in here and I'll say 'Good morning' to you, and you'll say 'Good morning' to me, just like they do in primary school.

KELLY   *(Putting up her hand)* Sir . . .

ALAN   And if anyone so much as opens their mouth they'll

find themselves standing outside Mrs Harrison's office.
Is that clear?

KELLY    Yes, Sir.

ALAN    Right, now we'll go and line up outside.

(*They do so. Alan follows them out.*)

Now we'll just wait here until everyone's standing
quietly.

(*Pause as they all stand uncomfortably.*)

KELLY    What's the matter, Sir?

ALAN    (*Menacing*) Did you say something, Kelly?

KELLY    (*Trying to make a joke of it*) Just thought you might have
gone crazy or something.

ALAN    You'll see just how crazy I can go if you push me any
further! (*Arthur is out of line.*) I said a straight line,
Arthur!

(*Arthur shuffles back into line.*) Now shall we go in and try
again?

(*They file into the classroom and stand by their chairs. Arthur
starts to sit, then stands as he sees everyone else is standing.*)

Good morning 4F.

STUDENTS    Good morning, Mr Howman.

ALAN    Thank you, you may sit, quietly! Take out pens and
paper and we'll have a little dictation.

THERESA    (*Whispers to Kelly*) Is this a test?

ALAN    Did I hear 'Is this a test?'? What a very good idea.
We'll make this a very special dictation test, just for
Theresa.

KELLY    Good idea!

ALAN    Shut up, Kelly!

(ARTHUR's **hand goes up.**)

I'll read everything twice and twice only. I'll also include commas, full stops and other punctuation – Arthur, put your hand down!

(*Alan begins to dictate.*)

'In the distant village . . . in the distant village . . .' Put your hand down Arthur, I'm only going to say this twice . . .

(ARTHUR's **hand goes down.**)

'We heard the tolling of a bell, comma . . . we heard the tolling of a bell . . . comma.'

(KELLY **whispers to her neighbour. ARTHUR's hand goes up again.**)

Shut up, Kelly! 'Cold, comma, sodden boots in wet grass . . . cold, comma, sodden boots in wet grass comma . . .' Arthur, if you don't know something, leave a space.

(ARTHUR's **hand stays up. That was not his problem.**)

'Rain trickling down our necks . . . rain trickling down our necks . . .' I said leave a space, Arthur, and put your hand down before I throw something at you!

(ARTHUR's **hand goes down.**)

'. . . we pressed forward in the darkness . . . we pressed forward in the darkness . . .'

(ARTHUR's **hand is up again. ALAN ignores it. Arthur desperately needs to go to the toilet but he doesn't dare to say so.**)

ALAN '. . . ignorant of the unseen horror . . . ignorant of the unseen horror . . .'

(ARTHUR **puts his hand down, then suddenly holds his head in his hands, very distressed.**)

'. . . that sooner or later . . . that sooner or later . . .'

(KELLY **notices what has happened to** ARTHUR. **The word spreads around the class. Everyone looks across at Arthur.** ALAN **slams down his book.)**

What the hell's going on? What are you playing at?

KELLY   It's Arthur, Sir.

ALAN   What is it, Arthur?

KELLY   Sir!

(ALAN **discovers the awful truth.)**

ALAN   Get out, the rest of you.

TRACY   Where will we go, Sir?

ALAN   I don't care, just get out!

(The CLASS **exits.** ARTHUR **remains, head down, close to tears.** ALAN **is quite unable to cope with the situation.)**

ARTHUR   I didn't mean to do it, Sir.

ALAN   I know that . . . er, would you like to go home? I'll explain to . . . who have you got after lunch?

ARTHUR   The others would only say that I . . .

ALAN   Don't worry what the others say. They're not worth worrying about.

(Pause. KELLY **appears at the door. She carries some tracksuit bottoms.)**

ALAN   I'm really sorry, Arthur.

(He notices KELLY.)

What are you staring at?

KELLY   I just brought some tracksuit bottoms for Arthur.

ALAN   Oh.

(He moves to take them from her but she pushes past him and hands them to Arthur herself. ARTHUR pulls them on over his trousers.)

Come on, Arthur, I'll give you a lift home.

ARTHUR    It's all right, Sir. I'll walk home.

(ARTHUR limps off. ALAN looks after him, still wondering whether to follow Arthur or leave him alone.)

KELLY    He'll be all right, Sir, I reckon. You should've let him go before he did it. Arthur's got this problem . . .

ALAN    I know, Kelly. So I made a mistake, OK? Everyone else makes mistakes – why shouldn't I? I'm only human.

(He sinks down in a chair, turning his face away from her. Long pause, then . . .)

KELLY    Hey, you're a good bloke, Sir.

(ALAN turns to see if she is kidding. She isn't. Music starts quietly.)

When are we going to do drama again, Sir?

ALAN    We'll see.

(KELLY smiles. ALAN smiles back and they exit together. As they go, Alan removes his tie.)


**The end**

# THE MAKING OF THE PLAY

## Notes on staging the play

*Cast size*

The play was originally written to be performed by a cast of four, playing multiple roles. Some new roles have been added to make the play more suitable for performance by a larger group, but the script also contains suggestions as to how the cast could be cut back to four if necessary.

In addition to the speaking parts, there are many sections of the play which offer possibilities for non-speaking group work. The action takes place in a big, overcrowded school, and nearly every scene could be played against a background of a jostling mass of teachers and students. The feeling of lack of privacy so created would help to suggest the pressure under which the main characters are working.

*The set*

Since the play was originally devised as a touring Theatre-in-Education piece, the set for the original production was minimal. I think it would be wise to keep settings as simple as possible, as they were in the original production. Because most of the things required for props – desks, dusters, blackboards and so on – are readily available in most schools, it may be tempting to use too many of them. The trouble here is that once a realistic staffroom, say, has been set up on stage, it takes too long to clear it off again. Most scenes are short, and the action needs to move quickly between them.

The set for the original production consisted of light aluminium cubes – small ones for chairs, larger ones for desks. Arranged in a row they represented a classroom. The desk cubes joined together made a long staffroom table and piled on top of each other they suggested display cases in the museum. The audience sat on three sides of the acting area.

We also surrounded the acting area with an aluminium cage, rather like the ones in which lion tamers operate inside the circus ring. This had some symbolic significance of course, but it also allowed us to play all the indoor scenes inside the cage and the 'corridor' scenes in the space between the cage and the audience.

*Topical references*

The play contains references to pop groups and film or television actors and attempts to use up-to-date teenage slang. These things change so fast that it is impossible to keep them all current. If you are producing the play, look carefully at each scene to see what is supposed to be happening in the relationships between the characters, but then feel free to embellish the text, bring it up to date and localise the slang. It is meant to be about a school in your area today!

## Original production

*The Fourth Year are Animals* (originally *Year 9 are Animals*) was devised with actors from Toe Truck Theatre, Sydney, Australia, and first performed by that company at St Peter Chanel School, Regents Park, New South Wales, on 25 February 1981, with the following cast:

| | |
|---|---|
| ALAN HOWMAN | Ian White |
| MARIE FORBES | Christine James |
| KELLY McCARRIE | Jean Kittson |
| ARTHUR MORAN | David Kerslake |
| SYLVIA HARRISON | Christine James |
| LES WILLIS | David Kerslake |
| THERESA CARETTI | Christine James |

The production was directed by Richard Tulloch.

*Richard Tulloch*

## FOLLOW-UP ACTIVITIES

## Role play

*The Fourth Year are Animals* aims to help students to see school from the teacher's point of view. Drama activities can be very useful in structuring 'role reversal' games to aid this understanding. There are many ways in which this can be done, but here are some suggestions:

(1) Let a number of students decide on a 'lesson' to be taught to the rest of the class. Each student prepares a lesson plan to teach the material in the most interesting and exciting way. Each student in turn then plays the role of the teacher for a few minutes, while the class, perhaps including the real teacher, try to respond as they normally would. After each attempt, the 'teacher-student' explains the objectives of the lesson, while the 'class' criticise the approach and suggest improvements.

(2) Following a number of mock classes of this kind, the 'teacher-students' could try to stage a staffroom discussion in which they talk about what went wrong in their classes and different approaches they could try.

(3) To show how the same event can be viewed from different points of view, select either one of the mock classes, or a scene from the play, or the 'Mummy's Tomb' lesson or the final scene in which Alan becomes disciplinarian, and ask a number of students to describe it as if they were one of the protagonists. This could be done in writing, but might perhaps be more spontaneous if each student decided to be Alan, or Arthur or Kelly or Theresa, and described the events as if speaking on the telephone to a friend. These conversations could be recorded on cassette, then played back and discussed.

(4) Try setting up scenes which are not included in the play – for instance:
   (i)   Les Willis complaining to the headteacher about Alan's lessons.
   (ii)  Les Willis teaching a maths class.
   (iii) Alan teaching his 4F English class following the end of the play.

In all these games, it is important for the classroom teacher to try to 'cast against type'. If one student always seems to be playing the role of the tough kid or the authoritarian teacher, try to get him or her to change roles for a while with someone who seems to be playing completely different characters.

## Discussion starters

(1) *Quote* (pp.43–4)

> MARIE    It's people like Les who survive . . .
>
> Teachers can't be brilliant and creative all the time. . .

(i)    In what ways do some students 'try out' new teachers?

(ii)   Many students say that new teachers give them more freedom at first and then 'get tough'. If this is so, what forces teachers to become disciplinarians?
Is this what happens to Alan in the play?

(2) *Quote* (p.42)

> ALAN    I can't teach kids if I have no idea who they are, what they're like and what they want.
>
> LES     They don't know what they want.
>
> ALAN    Have you ever asked them?
>
> LES     I know what they'd say – 'sex and drugs and rock and roll'.

Do students know what they want? Do students know what they need? Are schools giving them what they really need?

(3) *Quote* (p.43)

> LES     I'm not ashamed to say I don't understand kids at all. But I've found one thing, Alan, that I *can* do bloody well. I can teach kids so that they go out of my classroom knowing more than when they came in.
>
> ALAN    Whether they like it or not.
>
> LES     I don't care whether they like it or not. If they want a friend they can go out into the playground and find someone their own age to play with. All I need is their respect.

(i)    Is it possible to be a good teacher without understanding kids?

(ii)   Is it enough for a teacher just to know the subject matter?

(4) *Quote* (p.37)

> ALAN  And what are you going to do for the rest of your life? . . . What do you think's going to happen to you, eh?
>
> KELLY  Don't care.

Does Alan push Kelly too far when he questions her?
Is he 'taking an interest' or invading her privacy?

(5) *Quote* (p.25–6)

> LES  . . . good teaching is based on good routines . . . Now this 'Myths, Magic and Mummies' of yours is only going to upset the scheme of things. And when that happens, that's when the little piranhas take advantage.

(i)  Do students learn better when there is order and routine?
(ii)  How flexible should schools be to allow lessons like Alan's 'Mummy's Tomb' class to take place?
(iii)  Why did Alan try the lesson?

(6) *Quote* (p.49)

> KELLY  . . . You should've let him go before he did it. Arthur's got this problem . . .
>
> ALAN  I know, Kelly. So I made a mistake, OK? Everyone else makes mistakes – why shouldn't I? I'm only human.
>
> KELLY  Hey, you're a good bloke, Sir.

(i)  What happens when teachers admit their mistakes and let students see that they are human?
(ii)  How can this affect students' level of respect for teachers?

**Suggestions for further reading**

BRAITHWAITE, Edward, *To Sir, with Love* (Bodley Head)
CHUKOVSKY, Kornei, *Silver Crest: A Russian Boyhood,* transl. from Russian (OUP)
HINES, Barry, *Kes* (Heinemann)
HUNTER, Evan, *Blackboard Jungle* (Constable)
JAMES, Clive, *Unreliable Memoirs: Autobiography* (Cape)
PEYTON, K. M., *Pennington's Seventeenth Summer* (OUP)
RICHARD, Adrienne, *Into the Road* (Gollancz)
WARNER, Sylvia Ashton, *Teacher* (Virago)
WILLIAMS, Emlyn, *George: Early Autobiography* (Hamish Hamilton)